Style Code

Be More You. Look the Part. Feel Attractive.

Your Personal Guide to Image Confidence

Sola Adelowo, AICI FLC
Certified Image Consultant

ISBN-13: 978-1484931127

ISBN-10: 1484931122

Acknowledgements

My brother, Adebowale Adedayo Adelowo, an incredibly wise little cheetah. I miss you. Thanks for the lessons.

My grandfather, Chief Joel Sola Adelowo, a teacher, headmaster, and elder statesman who taught me to use my education and life experiences to help others find meaning in their own lives. Your torch lives on in America.

My parents who taught me "to whom much is given, much is expected."

My clients, mentors and friends – thanks for having faith in me.

To the reader, I remember the frustrations of not knowing what to wear for an occasion; where to begin to pull together a look that's truly you; or how to make sure your appearance is appropriate for all your roles. My gift to you is a clearer path to be intentional, be free and be more you.

Contents

Foreword

I've known Sola for several years, and I wanted to write this foreword for a simple reason: I admire her. She is a woman who makes it clear to me there are great leaders among us. I have watched her successfully navigate the challenges and successes of being the Founder and CEO of ImageCube with grace and dignity. She is relentlessly committed to the well-being of her clients and sincerely works to find solutions which last. I have been blessed to have her as a friend and a confidant.

She has helped me refine my image and better embrace my own style quirks, and made it possible for me to explain to others what I'm seeking to accomplish while presenting an appearance to support my statements. I hope, as you read this book, you discover something new about yourself. I hope you come away with new questions and a better sense of who you are today – and who you want to be tomorrow.

It is my personal belief there is no one more capable in the image and personal-branding industry than Sola Adelowo. No one else I can think of who puts as much heart into her work.

Do yourself a favor: work with her to make the best possible you visible to the world every day.

With sincere gratitude,

Phoenix R. Cavalier
Founder and CEO
Verus Branding

Sola Adelowo

Introduction

My hope is for you to use this book as a tool to find that your persona is not about clothing. It is about your internal voice. It is about feeling. When we feel good about our appearance, we put others at ease. I did not come to this understanding overnight, and I certainly can't take all the credit for what I've achieved thus far. In my case, I was blessed with a unique upbringing which illustrated and reinforced the importance of personal presentation.

I was born in Dallas, Texas, to my lovely Nigerian parents. However, I was raised for much of my childhood in Nigeria while my parents received their undergraduate and graduate degrees in the United States. Most of my attire was handmade by a tailor in Nigeria. My maternal grandmother was a fabric merchant and I was struck by the richness in the fabrics people wore. At an early age, I gained a vivid awareness of the power of presentation on the observer. At the core exists a cultural desire to honor both oneself and whomever you might encounter in your day. Fine fabrics and colorful, well-tailored clothing helped shape my interest in the power of a purposeful, personalized wardrobe. And yet, before I could help others, I had to complete my own journey of self-discovery.

I worked more than a decade for Chubb insurance, managing executive liability to help directors and officers protect company assets. I developed a team and was accountable for the profitability and growth of my division. What made me strong in this career was my sincere desire to help and teach insurance agents. What made me stand out was my keen awareness of how others experienced me. Even though I did well in my career at Chubb, I longed for a way to combine my cultural upbringing with my people skills and desire to make a difference in the lives of those around me. Friends and coworkers later would tell me, "I could really see you in a career that is fashion oriented …" or "ImageCube just makes more sense for you." With a BA in Sociology from Wellesley College, MBA coursework from Post University, and more than a decade in the corporate world, I finally was able to incorporate my practical awareness of corporate culture, business acumen, and social dynamics to create a process that makes fashion a relevant solution for professionals on all levels.

In 2008, I launched ImageCube. I spent time volunteering with Dress for Success of Indianapolis and I loved being part of such an empowering organization. Could I transition from a career in corporate America to running my own company? Yes! I researched stylists, image consultants, and various other fashion-centric industries. The *Conselle Institute of Image Management*, founded by Judith Rasband and AICI, the *Association of Image Consultants International*, where I would later earn my Certified Image Consultant status, were instrumental during this time of transition and new beginnings.

What I discovered as I studied, took tests, and completed dozens of different forms and "style surveys" was much of the fashion industry was so intent on packaging, they forgot about the person. In a world of makeovers and quick fixes, I was as overwhelmed as the next person by the number of options, trends, HOT Lists! and NOT Lists! I also researched personal development industries, including leadership coaches, and discovered experts so focused on behaviors and thought processes, they assumed the packaging was irrelevant to the person's credibility. There were two worlds – fashion and personal development industries – which were intent on serving the same person with incomplete processes. The challenge became how would I combine what I learned as a child with my sociology degree and professional experience to create a system anyone could use to harness the power of their authentic "look"?

This book is meant to help you find your voice and better express your personality while still aligning with your personal and professional goals.

You will find **clarity** in your buying decisions, **confidence** in your daily presentation skills, and **growth** in your ability to develop your image to match your evolving lifestyle.

With my very best wishes for
your ultimate image,

Sola

Sola Adelowo, AICI FLC
Founder of ImageCube, LLC.

My mother and her friend.

My parent's wedding day.

My Grandmother is my style icon. She knew how to make an entrance.

My Grandfather taught me leadership.

My fourth birthday in Nigeria. My paternal grandmother had my outfit made and dressed me in her jewelry. My maternal grandmother provided the fabrics. My maternal aunt made my birthday cake.

This photo was taken at my Grandfather's wake. I'm wearing my Grandmother's head wrap (gelé), which is made from stiff fabric that bends easily. Our family accent colors were orange and gold.

Various family members during the wake for my Grandfather. Women wearing beautiful gelés.

Me, my brother, Wale, and my mother's family.

Appearance is important in our culture. Our family with the Oba (king) of Ikirun [gentleman in white garb & white hat, holding the toddler] and his chiefs. Paying our respects for attending my Grandfather's services.

Going to the market to choose fabrics was part of everyday life. With colors and patterns varying widely, all designed by hand.

Sola Adelowo

Chapter One

.

Appearance Starts on the Inside

"When you consider the power of presentation, you know there's more to getting dressed than simply putting on clothes." — Sola Adelowo

This story makes clear how internal our outward presentation truly is.

Elana grew up in a culture where women are not allowed to cut their hair. Except for a trim to the edges, she had never been to a hair stylist, never considered a new hairstyle, and couldn't imagine herself looking different than smartly dressed with long, beautiful, dark brown hair.

While her upbringing had taught her to care for and appreciate her hair, she had never been invited to express her own sense of style through her appearance. When I met her, Elana had a degree in biology and a life unfolding in a positive way. She was at the crossroads of doing what she'd always done or changing to something new and — in many ways, unsettling.

She was considering getting her first haircut. Ever.

She had decided to book an appointment for a completely new hairstyle. She was ready to let what was becoming true for her on the inside become visible to others. The work we did together made her transformation gentle, patient, and moderate. Because her internal world had changed, her appearance needed a change as well. Elana needed balance between honoring her upbringing and honoring herself. We found new colors and textures to add to her wardrobe and worked with the hair stylist to create a change that maintained her comfort level.

Conversations were very meaningful for Elana and me. I learned once again how internal the process is for everyone. When we seek to do more than just put on clothes, we find a way to communicate who we are, what we value, and perhaps where we want to go in the future. This is why I created the **Image³ Style System**® as a way to help people before they rush to the nearest store in search of a new persona. The trick is to align what you know about who you are today, with where you are going in the future. Basing the journey on a scientific model, you avoid the "trend vacuum" and find your own personal **Style Code**® to capture how you like to look and feel, which will benefit you for years to come.

Confidence: You Don't Buy It, You Build It

It's true. Some people seem more confident than others. This doesn't mean you can't learn methods for exuding confidence even if you're a little shy or unsure. At the forefront of how people express confidence is their personal demeanor. Another facet is rooted in presentation details and overall packaging. From the color of a tie to a haircut, confidence has much to do with the way lines, colors, shapes, and proportions together send a clear message of authority, confidence, and credibility. Picture two men:

- *One wears a dark suit, a red tie, a gold watch, and has well-groomed hair. He gestures for you to sit and review a blueprint with him.*
- *The other man wears a red landscaping company polo, durable khakis, and steel-toed boots. He has the drafting plans for your project in one hand and your notes in the other.*

What these gentlemen have in common is the use of the color red. It is a commanding color and it signifies assertiveness and authority. The goal of exuding confidence is met when what you wear is aligned with your personal and professional intent. Picture the same two men in your mind and make the following changes:

- For the man in the suit, the tie is gone, and the dress shirt is now a plain white V-neck T-shirt.
- The landscape engineer is wearing a dirty hat and his shirt is an orange polo.

The change in color and texture redefines the tone. If you're seeking to raise your level of confidence and credibility, start with one thing you can control: visual perception. Your actions do the rest of the talking over time. It's about ensuring the message you send is the message you want people to receive.

This brings me to a story about a client who is a leader in her organization, but her presentation was undermining her ability to be taken seriously.

Janet's background includes professional ballroom dancing, which she still does from time to time. Her position as a Vice President of Operations demands decision-making and leadership. She came to a crossroads when she overheard the comment, "I just can't take her seriously."

Our work together revealed the flowing garments she wore were not supporting her leadership role. It was noted her presentation included a free-form hairstyle and somewhat casual shoes. She had received feedback that being around her was reminiscent of Woodstock or a Grateful Dead concert. While she was well liked, she wasn't garnering the respect she needed to do her job well. It all came down to lacking the understanding of how to align her message with her appearance.

Our results included buying clothes with clean lines and fewer frills, while maintaining accessories which offered the whimsy and flourish of texture she preferred. As someone whose personality embraced dancing and movement, it was important to include those elements.

The results were almost immediate for Janet. Her meetings and conversations led to faster action from members of her team. She still felt like herself through the accessories, but now she was receiving the attention she needed to thrive in her career.

You will express confidence in various ways in a single day depending on the job or task you perform. Confidence is easier to exude consistently when you have a plan for presenting yourself to others. This brings us to an important foundation for your image awareness: your roles and goals, and aligning what you say with what it *appears* you are saying.

Be More You: Roles and Goals

Your lifestyle influences how you dress. Any kind of key change will cause an internal transformation of who you are, today. Have you:

- Avowed to become more outgoing? Social? Recognized in the community?
- Committed to pursue a promotion at work or make a career move?
- Assumed a new role at work whereby your audience or duties have changed?
- Had a dramatic change in weight, up or down?
- Experienced the passing of a loved one recently?
- Watched the kids go off to college?
- Recently married your sweetheart or parted with the former love of your life?
- Moved to a new city?
- Celebrated a milestone birthday?

If you answered yes to one of these questions (or thought of your own recent life-changing event), you know the impact a major shift has on who you are today vs. the person you were. Take stock of the perception you want people to keep after meeting you.

We all are multi-faceted. Are you a leader? A supporter? A student? Along with professional roles, personal responsibilities also shape our persona. Problem solver, counselor, organizer, mentor, researcher, confidante, tutor, and so many more. This is why image is tricky when it's based on magazine clippings and trends without science to make the foundation strong. When you use the **Image³ Style System®** included in this book, you quickly determine what roles and goals to focus on as you refine and sharpen your persona so *you won't be guessing*. You'll have a plan connected to who you are, what you do, and where you want to take your life. This is about ensuring you're communicating deliberately every time you step out of your home and into the world. This helps you achieve your goals more quickly by garnering more control over the impressions you make.

Personal Brand: Define Your Core Message

Ask someone you know and trust to describe you in one word. This is the fastest way to gain an idea of how others "see" you. This simple step kicks off a new awareness of who you are to the world. Let's see how two people – Jennifer Aniston and LeBron James – present their personal brands:

- **Jennifer Aniston:** She became famous on TV and managed to inspire an entire culture of acceptance. Not being a tall bombshell, she chose to appear as an approachable person; the "girl next door" anyone could get along with. Instead of downplaying her casual appeal, she amplified it and remains an icon of cool, relaxed and approachable style.
- **LeBron James:** He offers intrigue by being taller and bigger than most. He goes beyond his athletic ability by giving back to his

community in a big and visible way. Inspiring others through his actions, he's taken advantage of his physical stature and used it to do good work, all while being a world-class athlete.

What these famous people have in common with *you* is the ability to positively apply personal traits toward a visual personal brand. What makes you stand out? What makes you memorable? If it's height, stand tall and be proud of it. If it's your wild hair, enhance its natural texture – add some highlights, get it styled, and make a statement. If it's your way with words or your quick wit, share these traits often.

When you think of branding, learn from companies. Consider Apple® and Microsoft®. Both present brand messages to appeal to a broad audience, while ensuring the core traits are intact. The common thread across all well-known brands is: they use consistent messages, themes and a signature logo and/or tag line.

This isn't to say you should rush out to trademark your name. It's to suggest when you create a vision for the brand you want to express through your image – be it sporty and thoughtful or serious and refined – you'll identify colors, shapes, and textures you want to adopt as your signature.

Personal Brand: Ready. Set. Go.

How do you want to be remembered after a meeting or social gathering? Practice on a regular basis, expressing what makes you unique. Through consistency and visibility you build trust and rapport with others. You'll establish your own compelling "personal brand." Identifying the elements you want to embrace allows you to create a vocabulary for yourself, expressing who you are in a comfortable manner for you.

Now that we've addressed some of the high-level ideas which brought you to this book, it's time to dive into the methods to make your life better from the tip of your favorite shoes to the top of your fedora. We'll consider several elements central to creating a "look," which is authentic and effective at helping you achieve what you want.

Here's what you'll need as you journey through your book:

- ✓ Red Pen: Underline ideas you want to implement in the next 7 to 14 days
- ✓ Blue Pen: Underline ideas you want to implement in the next 1 to 3 months
- ✓ Magazines: At least 3 current fashion, architecture, or interior design magazines to explore
- ✓ Scissors: Clip inspiring photos from your magazines
- ✓ Blank Paper: Use this to capture sketches, notes, and random thoughts
- ✓ Tech Savvy Alternative: Post inspiring images on your mood board in Pinterest, Polyvore, Tumblr, or other similar resource.

Sola Adelowo

Chapter Two

The Image³ Style System®

What you see below and on the next page is a high-level overview of how you benefit from the **Image³ Style System**® when you elect to create a one-on-one plan for redefinition and improvement. My approach is never about forcing a "hot new look" onto anyone. When we work together, we focus on what you want to achieve in your life in order to create a strategy for your best image. Let's consider the phases you will complete, if you were to begin a personal consultation with ImageCube.

1.	**Launch**	We begin with an in-depth personality assessment, which includes a greater number of variables than the model introduced in this book. It's a perfect way to gain insight about who you are internally, and it helps us create a path tailored within your comfort zone.
2.	**Goals**	We discuss your current roles, goals, lifestyle and the changes you want to make. This includes your near-, mid-, and long-term ambitions. We also talk about the audience you want to engage more often: be it a new community or a familiar one to whom you want to introduce a new you. We clarify your goals.

3.	Style Code®	Using tools like the assessment in this book, we'll find the adjectives that describe you and what colors, textures and other details support, enhance, and refine your Style Code. This is our filter as we find what works for you and how you like to look and feel.
4.	Preferences	We work together to find out what lines, shapes, textures, colors, and/or patterns match the goals you have for yourself. This is an excellent part of the process because you discover something you love is more relevant in a new way.
5.	Color Analysis	The colors you wear say a lot about you, which is why they must be chosen with care. By taking a serious look at the colors that reinforce your attractiveness, we begin minimizing certain colors from the list to define your style over time.
6.	Wardrobe	Knowing your Style Code, preferred styles, goals, and how others need to experience you, we review your wardrobe to see if you have the right tools. This allows us to keep what suits you and remove items that don't support your purpose.
7.	The List	Armed with new information and knowledge about what does and does not support your goals, we build your shopping list. It guides you on a regular basis, helping you stay away from clothes that won't help you enhance your image.
8.	Humility	ImageCube believes you know best, which is why guidance is offered, while working at the pace that is best for you. Instead of feeling you must start over, I will help you make decisions about your image from a position of strength. This is a process, and you always are in charge.

ImageCube is focused on helping you connect who you are inside with who the world sees. We cherish each discovery in your wardrobe as if it were a precious gem. Each garment, purse, or long-lost favorite sweater helps bring your story and personality assessment into focus, which in turn allows us to build an authentic plan.

Before we continue, I must share a story which demonstrates the importance of presenting yourself in a naturally appealing manner:

When a person approached my grandfather regarding a job opportunity, it was with good intentions, and he always was kind. However, if a person didn't present a polished, well-groomed appearance, my grandfather would say only five words, "Come back when you're ready" and he'd continue reading his paper. He viewed his brief counsel as a benefit to the person who was listening. He understood that to be ready, a person should look the part from head to toe, from the beginning. Often, the person would return and thank my grandfather for the honest feedback and the newfound understanding of the impact of personal presentation.

I won't suggest my grandfather was liked at the moment he rejected someone based on appearance. My grandfather was very clear about what someone should bring to the conversation through his or her appearance. Just consider how much power we each possess to begin every conversation from a solid, confident foundation.

Personal Reflection Break

The story about my grandfather is important because it asks us to consider the power of appearance and the role image plays in making our best impression. With a little fine-tuning and expert advice, you'll harness the ability to make every impression consistently strong. After all, it's like my grandfather taught me: if you're ready, you must look ready from the start.

Can you recall a time when you wished you had dressed more sharply?

_____

_____

_____

_____

Was there a time when you wanted to help someone but were distracted by his or her appearance?

_____

_____

_____

_____

Do you remember a time when you felt totally confident, from head to toe, about your presentation? Describe that moment.

_____

_____

_____

_____

_____

_____

_____

_____

_____

_____

_____

Chapter Three

Discover Your Authentic Image: What are your goals?

It's been said people make decisions about a new acquaintance in the first 30 seconds to 2 minutes of interaction. This does not give you much time to make a good impression, which is why sending the right message through your appearance is a function of having a clear understanding, acceptance and awareness of your goals, lifestyle and body type. You can use this awareness to select items which look appealing on you. When you think about fashion and style, the terms might be a bit vague. Consider two simple rules from the June 2010 issue of *MORE Magazine* online, as written by Shirley Yanez:

1. *Style equals confidence, not fashion.*
2. *Style is free; fashion is costly.*

Your image consists of the ways you use various elements of design to convey your personal style. Over time, it is how others know you. Your current identity may have been crafted by default, created by a dress code at work or put together without a clear vision. Now is the time to be more purposeful with your appearance. With the tools in this book, you'll craft your image intentionally.

The **Image³ Style System®** is based on three principles – Authentic, Appropriate and Attractive – which are intrinsically connected to your **Goals, Lifestyle and Body Type.**

Ask yourself a few questions about how well your appearance connects with your ambitions. Now let's go further by connecting your Goals, Lifestyle and Body Type into three principles of the **Image³ Style System®** that will guide your style choices.

AUTHENTIC is about appearing true to your GOALS: Think about your personal and professional aspirations and an event in the coming weeks which presents an opportunity to make positive impressions to move you closer to the picture you want to present. *Is it dating, social or influential?* You might need fabrics with more movement, texture or bolder patterns. *Is it numbers and authority?* You may need more structure, subtle movement, and subtle patterns.

APPROPRIATE is about appearing respectful to the audience in your LIFESTYLE: Think about your lifestyle and consider your audience – the people with whom you interact most often. *Where do you spend most of your time? What are you doing most of the time?* These factors correlate to the percentage of wardrobe supporting that part of your life.

ATTRACTIVE assures your clothes and accessories fit and flatter your BODY TYPE: Think about what you are wearing now and ask yourself if it makes you feel confident. You'll want more of that feeling. *Are people looking where you want them to look? Are you receiving positive compliments?*

Think through these three categories when you consider making a purchase. It starts with expressing your self-assuredness. Remember, *"Style equals confidence."* It implies self-assuredness in who you are, what you stand for, and your comfort in attracting positive attention. If the apparel doesn't support your GOALS, LIFESTYLE and BODY TYPE, skip it!

Personal Reflection Break

Use these types of questions to identify your goals:

Where do I see myself in five years; what is my plan to get there?

_____

_____

_____

_____

_____

_____

_____

What words or phrases best describe three attributes which distinguish me from others?

_____

_____

_____

_____

_____

_____

_____

What strengths, qualifications, expertise, specific skills or capabilities stand out most for me, and why?

_____

_____

_____

_____

_____

_____

_____

_____

_____

_____

Personality: The Characteristics You Regularly Express

First, it is vitally important to know that an understanding of your personality is just as important as a clear awareness of your goals. Your personality is comprised of the characteristics and natural tendencies you carry with you every day, everywhere you go. When you think about your own personality it can be difficult to be objective. How you see yourself may not be how others experience you, which is why we use an independent personality tool to help people just like you gain needed self-awareness. When you use personality tools, you gain insight measurable against a high volume of data. This invites a thoughtful review of what motivates you, and helps reveal how well your personality aligns with your personal and professional goals. These tools often help people make decisions about major life changes such as whether or not to remain in a certain career.

At ImageCube, we use the Myers Briggs (Personality) Type Indicator® (MBTI) with every client. The MBTI requires certified practitioners to interpret your results. That said, there are other trusted and self-administered options available online, which don't require a certified practitioner to interpret your results. For the purposes of this book, we encourage you to use the Keirsey Temperament® assessment, which is similar to the principles of the MBTI. MBTI has sixteen (16) personality types. The Keirsey model has four (4) temperaments. Each temperament corresponds with four MBTI personality types. For the purposes of this book's self-guided journey, the Keirsey Temperament® is an ideal tool. You can complete your own online assessment today with the information below.

Use the Keirsey Temperament® online assessment to align your personality with your image.

Complete your own personality temperament online at: www.keirsey.com. (last visited April 1, 2013).

How We Interpret The Four Keirsey Temperaments

GUARDIANS	*IDEALISTS*
Speak mostly of their duties and responsibilities, of what they can keep an eye on and take good care of, and they're careful to obey the laws, follow the rules, and respect the rights of others.	*Speak mostly of what they hope for and imagine might be possible for people. They want to act in good conscience, always trying to reach their goals without compromising their personal code of ethics.*
ARTISANS	*RATIONALS*
Speak mostly about what they see right in front of them, what they can get their hands on, and they do whatever works, whatever gives them a quick, effective payoff, even if they must bend the rules.	*Speak mostly of what new problems intrigue them and what new solutions they envision. Always pragmatic, they act as efficiently as possible to achieve their objectives, ignoring arbitrary rules and conventions if need be.*

Personality: Embrace Who You Are In All Aspects of Life

Rescue yourself from passionless work by integrating what you love about life with what you do for a living. Meet Marie.

Marie works in finance. In spite of her success, she was missing a connection between who she was internally and what she did for a living. Her true passions were art, pottery, and fine wine. She studied how wine was grown and cultivated, and took classes on wine becoming an investment opportunity.

Every morning when she looked in her closet, she saw a sea of grey, black and various shades of tan. She felt underwhelmed as she got dressed. Her image wasn't expressing who she was in an authentic way, and her professional role in a banking environment made her feel trapped by a career-based dress code.

Working with Marie allowed us to reveal her disconnect was a real and growing threat to her long-term prosperity and happiness. It turned out her Myers-Briggs® personality type was ENFP (Idealist), which describes a person who is Extroverted I'N'ntuitive Feeling and Perceiving. ENFPs have the ability to inspire and motivate others; ironically these personality traits are not common in careers in finance.

ENFPs thrive on high energy in life, color in fashion, and have a strong need for aesthetic stimulation. The excitement missing from her closet was missing from her successful career. After working together, we found a way for Marie to integrate her passion for fine wine with the work she does for her financial clients. In the past, Marie had held quarterly workshops in her branch office to share investment advice. After considering how she wanted to look and feel, we created a strategy to combine Marie's personal passions with her wealth of knowledge in the financial industry.

Instead of holding another workshop in her branch office, Marie would host unique wine-tasting events, with financial advice added throughout each gathering. Several years ago she purchased an exciting and stylish crimson-red Bolero jacket while traveling in Spain, but she had never worn it. For Marie, the combination of what she loved in life and what she did for a living created an opportunity for her to finally wear the stylish jacket and deepen her relationship with her clients, while differentiating herself professionally. Sharing knowledge and insights about wine and finance, while wearing her favorite red jacket, Marie found herself enjoying her clients and her work more.

Marie was experiencing harmony between what she did for a living and who she was as a person. This is what it means to be more YOU every day.

Style Choices by The Four Keirsey Temperaments®

The following chart represents (1) common comments of ImageCube clients about their style preferences and (2) recommendations on how to incorporate fashion trends – as they have been observed for each personality temperament.

GUARDIANS	IDEALISTS
prefer clothes which are …	prefer clothes which are …
1. … *no fuss, keep-it-simple styles*	1. … *very romantic, fluid, Bohemian*
2. … *on trend with current colors*	2. … *on trend with rounder shapes in prints and patterns, and softer fabrics*
ARTISANS	**RATIONALS**
prefer clothes which are …	prefer clothes which are …
1. … *dramatic, edgy, "Life is a stage – You're On!"*	1. … *geometric, intricate and detailed*
2. … *on trend with bolder, exaggerated shapes in prints and patterns, and intense textures*	2. … *on trend with modern shapes in prints and patterns, and subtle textures*

Imagine how these various personality descriptors take shape with individuals. Each person is naturally drawn to different shapes, colors, textures, patterns, and line quality. The importance of personality cannot be understated when creating an image which feels authentic, and – most importantly – within the comfort zone of how you like to look and feel. By working from the inside out, you aren't driven by "look-at-me" trends or "hot fashion tips." You build on a solid foundation of understanding who you are.

This returns us to the core reason for this book: helping you begin your journey with a clear connection to the person you are within. Understanding your internal world can make smart fashion choices easy. This is what makes ImageCube so powerful – YOU are at the center of every step.

What's Your Style Code?

Your Style Code is based on the adjectives you feel best describe how you like to look and feel, most of the time. Cut out images that you LOVE from fashion, architecture or interior design magazines, or create a mood board in online communities like Pinterest or Polyvore. These images will inspire how you choose multiple adjectives and narrow your selection to five (5) core traits. This is your self-guided Style Code; you'll use it as a filter to help you find the colors, textures, fabrics, patterns, and shapes you LOVE and are authentic for you.

Revisit your Style Code periodically to determine if it's still accurate. If it needs an update, revise it. If it doesn't need adjustments, you're good to go. By learning what is true for you about your self-image, you'll be better equipped to define what supports your personal and professional goals.

1. Check or circle the adjectives you believe best describe your selected images.
2. Write down additional adjectives that suit your images.
3. In cases where adjectives are used more than once, place a check for each time the same adjective is used.
4. Choose five adjectives you used most often.
5. Write the five you've selected in the "My Style Code" box.
6. Select the three colors you like most.

☐ Vibrant	☐ Culture
☐ Elegant	☐ Pulled-Together
☐ Thoughtful	☐ Innovative
☐ Powerful	☐ Classic
☐ Feminine	☐ Athletic
☐ Effortless	☐ Flirty
☐ Sophisticated	☐ Modest
☐ Stylish	☐ Cheerful
☐ Cheerful	☐ Comfortable
☐ Bold	☐ Sensual
☐ Clean	☐ Artistic
☐ Tasteful	☐ Sporty
☐ Delicate	☐ Well-Designed
☐ Modern	☐ Sexy
☐ Fun	☐ Intriguing
☐ Complex	☐ Organize
☐ Colorful	☐ Smart
☐ Unique	☐ Accomplished
☐ Outgoing	☐ Friendly
☐ Subtle	☐ Adventurous
☐ Warm	☐ Versatile
☐ Easy Going	☐ Quirky
☐ Refined	☐ Vintage
☐ Creative	☐ Luxurious
☐ _____	☐ _____

MY STYLE CODE

Select Three Colors
You Like the Most:

☐ Red	☐ Black
☐ Orange	☐ Brown
☐ Yellow	☐ White
☐ Green	☐ Grey
☐ Blue	☐ Silver
☐ Purple	☐ Gold
☐ _____	☐ _____

Personal Reflection Break

Which personality temperament best describes you?

_____
_____
_____
_____
_____
_____

Describe the characteristics of the clothes you love to wear most:

_____
_____
_____
_____
_____
_____

What traits from one or more of the other temperaments would you care to adopt?

_____
_____
_____
_____
_____
_____

What colors, textures, shapes, or garment qualities would you care to add to your wardrobe?

_____
_____
_____
_____
_____
_____

Chapter Four

Discover Your Appropriate Image: What is your lifestyle?

What we think of as appropriate has more to do with where we're going, than where we're coming from. This is why what we wear has such a big impact on how people perceive us. At the heart of the question of appropriateness is the audience with whom we plan to engage. When you're headed to a party with friends, shorts and a printed T-shirt should be great. But, if it's an upscale garden party to celebrate your friend's engagement, wear more polished options like a sports coat and dress pants. The extra effort of wearing the coat and nicer pants subtly conveys respect for the occasion – it's not every day that your friend gets engaged! Appropriateness is all about your audience, and how well you understand their expectations and social customs. By aligning with your audience and your personal and professional goals, you're a step ahead before you step out the door. Knowing your audience allows you to present the right information in a manner valuable to the people you meet.

Consider Sandra, a client, who wasn't connecting with her audience at work in spite of her talent, experience and credentials.

Sandra said: I've been given feedback that I don't come across as a manager. What do you suggest I do so others perceive me as a manager and leader even if I'm not a fan of wearing suits and jackets?

Some elements of culture are too ingrained to be ignored. The strong shoulders of a jacket tell others in no uncertain terms, "I'm capable." It says you "shoulder" the weight of your responsibilities. It's not about wearing a jacket because you must; it's about wearing a jacket because it's part of your uniform as a leader. In a similar way, titles such as "Dr." or "MD" lend credibility and authority – a blazer boosts your perceived authority and makes it easier for others to believe you know what you're talking about. The good news is you don't have to go with a plain color or boxy shape. Look for subtle patterns or interesting textures to increase your level of approachability while maintaining an authoritative presence. Pay close attention to your posture as well. Keep your feet firmly planted, keep your back straight, shoulders down, and chin up. Speak from your diaphragm and use your tone to express confidence. These various elements, (appearance, posture, voice-tone) combine to present a cohesive professional presence. Remember, wearing a uniform doesn't mean giving up your authenticity. It means challenging yourself to express who you are from a another angle.

Sandra was challenged to connect with an audience that wasn't immediately recognizing her authority. She preferred to wear clothes that were "comfortable," including sweaters, sweatshirts, or mohair cardigans with T-shirts. She started to include in her wardrobe comfortable-feeling, structured knit jackets and cardigans in subtle versions of prints that she loves. By better aligning her image and presentation with her audience, her team started to listen to her and they were more willing to engage in conversations with her. The key to this adjustment was ensuring she retained her core personal style preferences and her edge. This came through her accessories, and through the textures and prints she chose for herself.

This brings us to YOU. **Think about this: how would your appearance change if you were selling a $3 million home versus a $57,000 home?** Would you present the same characteristics in both cases? As you think about this question, I am certain you're picturing what you'd wear, perhaps what you'd be driving. You may be aware your voice tone or communication style might be different as well. At the core of the differences is the fact your *audience* is varied. While there is less of a shift needed between homes which are about 5 to 10 percent apart in price, in the example above the gap is so significant you would need to shift your disposition to better connect with your audience in a deliberate, meaningful way.

Think about the 10 different environments listed below and picture in your mind how you might dress differently for each of them. Next, consider how you'd keep your unique sense of style intact, while presenting an image suitable to your target audience.

1. Work at a Bank
2. Work at an Architectural Firm
3. Work at a Health and Wellness Organization
4. Work in an Outside Sales Role
5. Work at a University / College
6. Attend a Networking Event
7. Attend a Fundraising Event
8. Attend a Sports Event
9. Enjoy a Night Out
10. Attend a First Date Night

The photo on this page is of a purple suit with a blouse and a "statement" scarf with rich patterns. The shoes are a low, pointed heel with a metal bow to maintain professional credibility. This outfit was created for a client who worked at a bank and was tired of wearing boring black or grey clothes. The goal was to find more colors, prints, and shapes that are still conservative enough for work while staying true to her personal style.

The solution worked for her because she was dressed for her target audience and her own enjoyment. She could now express her overall message in a way which worked with her environment, instead of fighting against it. This is the essence of wearing what you love and fitting in to your professional environment.

Personal Reflection Break

When you think of your own work environment and the social boundaries which are part of your industry, you see how fashion, image, and style options can be difficult to choose. If you're in a very creative industry, you may have more latitude. Even then, you must maintain your credibility. Thinking of your own situation, write answers to the questions below.

Describe the various roles, events, and functions that arise in your professional role.

_____
_____
_____
_____
_____
_____

How do you need to be perceived by others in the roles, at events, or at other functions?

_____
_____
_____
_____

What message do you think your image conveys to the world?

_____
_____
_____
_____

How does that image resonate with your aspiration or your desired professional goals?

_____
_____
_____
_____

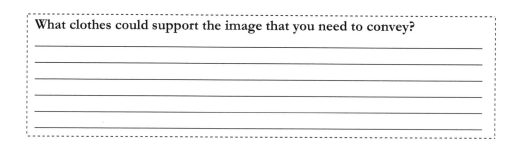

What clothes could support the image that you need to convey?

Chapter Five

Personal Expression with Color for Your Audience

A male client in his early 30s recently shared that, over the last year or so, he's started to wear a lot of purple. What makes him laugh is that he recalls a time when he never would have worn anything purple ... not one thing! Now he says he has six or more shirts in various shades of lavender, dark purple, and other interpretations of this royal hue. So what changed? It wasn't fashion magazines or pop culture, it was an internal change in who he was that led to an outside expression of color. The color matched a change in how he saw himself, and wearing it fulfilled an internal desire to be more expressive, which is why he now wears more purple.

Color is a way to amplify your image with emotional appeal. Through color you can express energy, enthusiasm, drive, and passion. Don't be shy about it. Start with a subtle use of color in a scarf, tie, or unique piece of jewelry. Color isn't about being brash; it's about the emotional qualities it contains. It helps to better communicate your emotional state. The beauty of color is the way it invites others to connect with you and allows you to share part of your story at the same time. Color is powerful to garner positive and thoughtful feedback to benefit you. Its use must be tempered with strategy.

Embrace Color to Share Your Authentic Story

The use of color takes on a personal meaning. My career history includes an extensive background in corporate environments where my persona needed to be compatible with CEOs *and* front-line employees. Balancing the demands of a personal image with professional goals invited me to choose a color palette suited to my personal style, while matching the tone of my work environment.

The photos you see on this page demonstrate how quickly color translates into different expressions of the same person. In each picture, I express my authentic professional self. The only difference is how I use color to connect with different audiences. What remains the same in both of these poses is the use of strong lines and shapes offered by a jacket. The differences are found in the tailoring of each garment, down to the softly textured buttons of the blazer on the right.

In the more reserved image on the left, I was an employee at Chubb Insurance company. My appearance was appropriate for the corporate culture and the clientele that Chubb served. I wore colors I preferred and which suit me (with a warm and subtle palette). Muted tones express warmth and solidity, and the blazer provides a subtle sheen which appears as texture. The shapes, muted color, and subtle print of the blouse offer visual interest, without being distracting.

In the more energetic photo on the right, I've chosen to amplify the once-muted colors, and present them in a brighter, more energetic way. By choosing tone-on-tone, I create a clear message of energy and enthusiasm. This connects with my ImageCube brand in a new way. One primary color expresses energy and joy; a whimsical strand necklace provides visual interest, while a white round-neck top, with a linear texture, adds layers without being bulky. You can do the same thing for your own image.

Below are three simple tips to help you amplify your brand message with a little color.

Choose Color Wisely: It's about a feeling, literally! Each color connects with people in an emotional and psychological way. For example, the color blue has been scientifically proven to calm the mind, and it ranks high as a trustworthy color. Before wearing red pants to the office, think about the color and its message. Taking an extra 5 minutes with this step can help you easily connect with people in a positive way.

One at a Time: While color is wonderful, too much of anything is dangerous. Focus on a three-element strategy to introduce color without over-doing it. First: choose a top, pant or jacket that amplifies the attractive colors of your hair, eyes, or skin tone. Second: harmony is found in a purse, scarf, tie or layering garment that pulls your look together. Third: focus on simple items which add a little shine to your overall appearance. This can be jewelry like a watch in silver or gold to match the coolness or warmness of your skin's undertone.

Be Expressive: The power of color is found in its ability to help everyone express themselves in a personally meaningful way. This is not about shouting out loud. It's about communicating deliberately through color choices which support your personal and professional goals. If you want to be taken more seriously at work, consider taking your love of orange to a calmer and more muted level. If you're in a creative work environment and you're not feeling valued, it may be time to ditch the navy blazer for a more vibrant blue.

Personal Reflection Break

No matter what your objectives, color can help you achieve them. When you think about your background, culture, upbringing, and lifestyle, you may notice certain color themes. These are evident in a color which was present in your home as a child. Other elements would have come from your environment, be it green mountains, white snow-covered hills, or tan and sunny beaches. These colors have subconsciously shaped your color palette.

Think of how you grew up, where you grew up, and the influences of family and friends. Describe the colors which fill your memories and make note of how certain colors make you feel.

_____

_____

_____

_____

_____

_____

_____

Chapter Six

The Science of Personal Image and Presentation

For many people, the big question is whether there is a scientific way to manage one's overall image, style, brand, and message. The answer is simple: YES. This is not a guessing game. Your personal goals, values, and your personality must be aligned with the style choices you make. If they are not, *who* you are and what you *present* are incongruent.

Proceed with caution when you approach the science behind fashion and the fundamental elements of design that support the constructing of clothing and accessories. The fundamental elements of design include lines, shapes, colors, textures, and patterns; we see these elements every day in nature and in our surroundings. How these elements combine communicates different meanings in our society. Think back to the last time you saw a movie. Before a character begins to speak you already knew the time of day based on the settings like daylight coming through the window or cereal bowls with milk on the table. You knew if the character had just woken up because she's wearing pajamas. You knew if she worked on Wall Street because of the darker color pinstripe suit. You knew if she was heading to a dance party because of her sparkly swingy dress. But if the plan was for a night at home without a date to read a book, you saw her wearing a cozy turtleneck with comfortable jeans covered with a blanket lying on the couch. The clothes speak. How the fundamental elements of design combine to create the dark pinstripe suit, sparkly swingy dress, cozy turtleneck and comfortable jeans, provides foresight into the imminent task. The same way you knew about the character and deduced her imminent task is the same way others make assumptions about you and your pending goals. *Your awareness of the science behind style is a great tool, but it is not a substitute to authenticity.*

The Science of Color

We'll start with a long list of the colors which – for good reason – make outfits stand out. Certain colors have a quality all their own. Cleopatra was very fond of the color purple. It has a long history of being enjoyed by royalty and is often viewed with an extra measure of appreciation for that reason. As you look through the list of traits and characteristics related to specific colors, think about the way you use color today. Ask yourself, "What would I do differently?"

NAVY	Honesty, integrity, trustworthy, hardworking, organized
BLACK	Sophisticated, high authority, power, assertive, mysterious, sensual
WHITE	Fresh, clean, hopeful, reliable, artistic, expressive
TAN/CREAM/CAMEL	Elegant, approachable, non-offensive, trusting

BROWN	Stable, secure, persevering, slow to change
RUST	Earthy, friendly, approachable
CHARCOAL GRAY	Strength of character, authoritative, refined
BURGUNDY/MAROON	Classic, refined, elegant, formal
PLUM	Regal, diplomatic, sophisticated
TEAL	Inventive, soothing, balancing
INDIGO	Creative, unusual, artistic, intuitive
RED	Dramatic, self-assured, active, high energy, courageous
ORANGE	Social, fun-loving, enthusiastic, thoughtful
YELLOW	Creative, outgoing, bright, cheerful, optimistic
GREEN	Nurturing, friendly, kind, peaceful, helpful
BLUE	Communication, logic, soothing, inspiring, honesty, patience, high ideals

VIOLET	Sensitive, unusual, psychic, spiritual, exotic, strong sense of inner direction
PINK	Quiet, refined, artistic, universal color of love, devoted to people and ideals
CORAL	Combination of pink and orange attributes
SILVER	Artistic color, creative, balanced
PERIWINKLE	Combination of indigo and violet attributes, quiet inner strength

The Science of Texture

When it comes to fashion, there's a time and place for wearing texture. Texture adds depth with very little effort. Have you noticed how a scarf, worn in the right way, makes a simple dress more elegant? Texture adds volume, interest, and drama to the shapes we see.

Texture can take an old favorite and give it a new life. Texture offers variety to a more muted color palette. Instead of feeling limited, add value to ordinary colors with rich textures. This adds visual interest to your overall presentation. Even a monochromatic look is more engaging when there are layers, lines, and weight to see and enjoy.

1. Smooth textures appear professional and provide surfaces which are often uninterrupted and cohesive, like wool or cotton.	**2.** Heavy texture appears informal and approachable and is seen in clothes like sweaters.
3. Subtle textures are more casual. Corduroys and tweeds have these types of texture.	**4.** Evening clothes appear formal and are usually shiny and tightly woven with the goal of gaining attention with sequins, brocades or jacquards.

Personal Reflection Break

Color and texture are dynamic tools for communication. They affect the people we meet, and in some cases determine the depth and quality of our interaction with others. It is generally understood some clothes are "Sunday clothes" and some are not. What you wear sets certain expectations from others (especially with first impressions).

Thinking of your current image, describe the textures you use, the colors, and the overall tone of your message. Make a note about what you want to retain going forward.

_____

_____

_____

_____

_____

_____

_____

_____

_____

_____

_____

_____

_____

_____

_____

_____

_____

_____

_____

_____

The Science of Line

When we talk about the science of lines, we're examining how the lines of clothes reinforce your body's boundaries. From a distance lines give a person's body its silhouette. In the way men in suits and women in dresses are immediately recognizable, lines communicate the nature or demeanor others perceive.

1. Vertical, straight lines suggest more authority and command attention. Think about pinstripes. People in traditional positions of authority – bankers and lawyers – often wear these types of lines.	**2.** Curved lines appear more approachable, less formal and tend to be considered less uptight or rigid.
3. Circular lines are playful and whimsical. Polka dots are another recognizable use of circular lines.	**4.** Meandering lines appear less predictable and more abstract. These lines are best suited for more creative professionals.

Patterns Create Formal or Informal Tones

With every choice, you'd like to understand the way your image comes into focus for the people you plan to engage. The goal of using a pattern is to create visual interest without being a distraction to others. Consider: a small checkered pattern on a shirt can be attractive, but wearing an entire suit with this design would be overwhelming.

1. Tiny or small patterns are non-active, almost non-descript and often are observed as one color.	**2.** Controlled, uniform patterns appear more professional than an abstract pattern.
3. Large patterns are lively, energetic and attention grabbing. Use caution as they can appear clownish.	**4.** Jacquards, hound's tooth, or herringbone are perceived more professionally than multi-colored patterns.

Details Finish an Outfit and Send a Clear Message

From the way a sock pattern is chosen to how neatly a beard is trimmed, details matter. These details are messengers for you, and you've no doubt put them to use in your own life.

Whether it was meeting your in-laws for the first time or seeking to hit it off during a big interview, you have spent time on the details. As you pay attention, you'll become clearer on what your clothes say about you and the image you project. When you create harmony between your words and presentation, you build trust and credibility, which is priceless.

Professional symbols mixed with casual symbols could make the right statement for a work situation. For example, a veterinarian needs to establish a more compassionate tone with families than a lawyer. Law and finance, however, share similar dress codes. The advertising and fashion industries are more fashion forward in order to connect with their creative service offerings. By knowing the symbols of clothing, you can create your own strategic plan for looking great from morning through evening, with little effort.

People look for certain symbols to assure them of your professionalism. How many people wear a Rolex watch (or the equivalent) because of its strong message of success?	PROFESSIONAL SNAPSHOT	CASUAL SNAPSHOT
	To be viewed more professionally, dress in a suit (including a jacket with a collar and lapels, and matching skirt or pants) worn with a dress shirt or blouse, plus dress shoes and accessories (belt, watch and scarf or tie).	To be viewed more casually, rely on casual symbols which include mix- and-match pieces. Instead of wearing a suit, mix a taupe pant with a black blazer. Add texture, use patterns and prints, and opt for multiple colors.

Symbols of Your Clothing Matrix

	PROFESSIONAL FORMAL	CASUAL INFORMAL
COLOR	Navy, grey, dark shades, high contrast, one or two colors	Light, bright, multiple colors, low to medium contrast
TEXTURE	Smooth fabrics, fine and tight weaves	Nubby tweeds, loose weaves, mix and match
PATTERN	Small or faint pattern with solid lines, not broken; no pattern	Floral prints, abstracts, big, wild
LINE	Vertical, straight	Curved, circular, meandering
WATCH	Metal band, fine leather	Sports or novelty watch
JEWELRY	Metal, no movement	Dangly earrings, charm bracelets, bangles
HANDBAG	Structured leather	Soft leathers, fabric
SHOES	Pumps, oxfords, close-toed flats	Open-toed sandals, tennis shoes,

Personal Reflection Break

With more of an awareness of the science behind the elements of fashion design, think about your primary goal – either personal or professional. Consider how this understanding can help you maintain your credibility and enhance your believability. Thinking of your own situation, answer the following questions:

Which design characteristics would support your goals?

_____

_____

_____

_____

_____

_____

How will clothes with these design details support your goals?

_____

_____

_____

_____

_____

_____

Describe how you can enhance your tone or help set a mood with what you wear.

_____

_____

_____

_____

_____

_____

Chapter Seven

Discover Your Attractive Image: What Is Your Body Type?

To convey a clear and confident message, choose clothes that fit your body type and direct attention where you need others to focus. You probably have seen a person wearing too many accessories or trying all the latest trends in one outfit. Looking at them is like going to the circus – you're not sure where to focus and it creates a confusing experience. A similar experience happens when you see a gentleman with a fuller belly and the buttons on his dress shirt are barely closing or a fuller busted woman in a dress shirt with buttons that barely close at her chest. You and everyone else will look at them and wonder if they didn't realize their buttons are not closing. You might even feel embarrassed if you accidently catch a glimpse of a bra. Well don't feel badly. These are examples of situations where the individual has not provided a clear focal point and is unaware of his or her body type.

To achieve your goals, you need others to focus people's attention on one to two focal points that are in close proximity to where you will convey your message. For giving a speech, the focal point should be near your face. This can be gained by wearing a bowtie, pin or colorful scarf. For date night, the focal points can be your curves which are accentuated by a curve-hugging wrap dress. Or you can accentuate and call attention to an athletic physique by wearing skinny or European-style jeans or dress shirts. But for modeling shoes, the smooth surface of waxed legs and polished toes direct attention to the focal point at the feet. In each scenario, there are one or two focal points in close proximity to where a message is being conveyed. To prevent distracting from the main message, all other clothes and accessories should be quiet. This is the essence of appearing attractive – in a manner that truly creates an aesthetically pleasing viewing experience.

Body type also can be a communication barrier if you choose clothes that appear unflattering. Ill-fitting clothes distract others from your message. You may have heard body types described as pear, apple, inverted triangle or hourglass – terms often used in fashion magazines. You may have determined your own body type based on these quick descriptors. The truth is most people are a combination of at least two body types. I'll use myself as an example.

Above the waist I have the broad shoulders and fuller bust of the "inverted triangle." I have a defined waist (the "hourglass" body type), but I also have the fuller buttocks (not hips) of a "triangle." When I shop for clothes, the first thing I do is accommodate my widest or fullest areas. If clothes fit where I'm the widest or fullest, they likely fit the rest of my body in a flattering manner.

These body areas typically present fit challenges for people:

- Neck, especially for men
- Shoulders
- Bust
- Chest
- Stomach

- Rise or Crotch (bellybutton to lower back)
- Buttocks
- Thighs

Body type is not a barrier when you create visual balance through the selections you make. Choose clothes with design details that draw attention to where you need attention and that will appear flattering on your body. Accommodate your fit challenge areas first to minimize a disturbing appearance. Choose clothes that provide balance by minimizing fullness or width, or you can create volume and weight on a slight frame.

Personal Reflection Break

Whether barriers are literal or psychological, it's critical to identify them and create a strategy to manage them. Barriers may include too many conflicting styles or ill-fitting clothing choices that undermine your credibility and distract from your message. These barriers can be career limiting or lead others to misunderstand your intentions.

Where do you need others to focus their attention?
Why do you need them to focus on your face, curves, legs, hands or feet ?

_____
_____
_____
_____
_____
_____

Thinking of images in fashion magazines, pay attention to how garments move and fit models. Ask yourself; "Would the neckline, waistband, hemline, etc., hit me in the same places on my body?" The models serve as a frame of reference to help determine if the proportions of the garment will enhance your own figure variations. It's not about comparing who has longer legs, bigger breasts or a smaller waistline. It is about the garment. What purpose would it serve in your wardrobe? If necessary, how could you adapt the garment to enhance your proportions?

When attending fashion events, ask questions such as, "How would I use the colors the model is wearing?" or "How might a new hairstyle support my professional goals?" You gain from an inside look at trends in clothing. Whether it's an updated interpretation or something fresh from a talented artist, ask yourself, "How can I use this to better connect my appearance with my preferred audience?"

Fit-and-Flatter Garment Guide

Blouses and Shirts	Skirts
✓ Neckline should fit around your neck without gapping or squeezing your neck. ✓ Buttons and zippers should close and be smooth on your chest and stomach. ✓ Be sure you can raise your arms and bend with enough ease to move comfortably. ✓ Bending over, your shirt or blouse shouldn't become revealing. ✓ Sleeves should come to the crease in your wrist when your arms are by your side.	✓ Fasten the waistband and ensure you can fit two fingers easily inside the band. ✓ Ensure you can sit without the skirt riding up or becoming revealing. ✓ Make sure skirts hang straight down from your fullest area (hips, stomach or thighs) and don't "cup" under your buttocks. ✓ Check that pleats, pockets, and vents are flat or closed without creating gaps or tension. ✓ Walk naturally to test that pleats are suited to your height and proportions.

Pants and Slacks	Jackets and Vests
✓ Be sure the waistband fastens comfortably around your waist, without pinching.	✓ Jackets must fit comfortably across your shoulders, bust, and chest without horizontal tension lines across the shoulders or vertical lines under the arms or down the spine.
✓ Pants should fall straight down from your fullest area, without tension.	
✓ Ensure there is enough rise (crotch to waistline) to accommodate the buttocks or crotch.	✓ Lapels should be flat and symmetrical on your body, and must not "stand up" on the body.
✓ Hemlines should skim the top of your shoe in front and heel in back.	✓ Side or center vents must be smooth without pulling horizontally or spreading when standing.
✓ Pockets and pleats must be closed and shouldn't 'pucker' or stand open when standing still.	✓ Be sure a jacket or vest fits over garments without becoming tight.
	✓ Raise arms to ensure seams aren't strained.

My hope is for you to begin seeing your body type as an asset. You can incorporate these guidelines to help make your goals a reality. You have resources all around you, and they're easier to see once you know what kind of assistance you need. What we present through our physical nature plays a large part in how people perceive us. Recognize you are in charge of initial perceptions. This is the power of harnessing your image and it's what ImageCube loves to help people do every day.

Personal Reflection Break

Making the most of your appearance isn't about throwing out all your clothes or going through some reality-show crash course. It's about evaluating simple things you can do to look and feel better each day as you move closer to your goals. Based on the Keirsey® model with four (4) temperaments, and the different needs of body types, it's clear every person has different needs based on their unique physical traits.

How would you describe your body type?

_____

_____

_____

Describe the characteristics that you like about your body.

_____

_____

_____

_____

_____

_____

What colors are your eyes, hair and skin?

_____

_____

_____

What clothes have presented fit challenges for you?

_____

_____

_____

_____

_____

_____

_____

_____

What comes to mind when you think about altering clothes as it relates to

---

your body type?

_____

_____

_____

_____

_____

_____

10 Tips for a Perfect Fit

Think back to a time you went shopping for new clothes and you asked yourself or a friend, "Does this fit?" This question is at the heart of personal confidence in one's image. The clothes we wear affect how we think, feel and act, and in turn, they affect how others react and respond to us. Perhaps you've seen a woman adjusting a too tight or too short skirt, or a man hitching up pants which were too loose or too long. The "wrong fit" makes us feel uncomfortable, self-conscious, and insecure – as if everyone were staring. Self-conscious behaviors caused by poorly fitting clothes undermine our professionalism. Use these 10 Tips whenever you're shopping:

1. **Her Suit**
   Jacket should hang straight or flare down below a woman's stomach. Her office-appropriate dress and skirt length is 2 to 2 ½ inches below the center of her knees. Her dress pant and slack hem should brush the top of her shoes.

2. **His Suit**
   Jacket should hang straight down below a man's stomach and cover his buttocks. A vest should be long enough to cover his waistband (for suspenders) or belt. His trouser and slack hem should brush the top of his shoes. A tie should be long enough to reach the top or middle of the belt buckle or top of the waistband (for suspenders).

3. **Try Three Sizes**
   Try on items in your size, a size above and a size below. The winner is

free of visible underwear outlines or edges.

4. **Get Physical**
   You're not a mannequin. Before you buy, view the garment in a three-way mirror as you bend, sit, stretch, and walk for a real-life perspective.

5. **Lines**
   As you try on clothes and move around, look for areas where the fabric pulls or bunches. When you see horizontal wrinkles, it means too tight. When you see vertical wrinkles, it means too loose or too big. When you see gapping or bulging, it means out of proportion with your body type. .

6. **Smooth Operator**
   Seams, closures, pleats and vents should lie smoothly.

7. **Rest Easy**
   Necklines, collars, lapels and pockets should lay flat – no gapping or visible undershirts or cleavage.

8. **Edge to Edge**
   Shoulders of a suit coat should extend one-half inch beyond your shoulder.

9. **Arm's Length**
   Long-sleeve shirts should end at the wrist with elbows bent. Dress shirt sleeves should extend one-quarter to one-half inch beyond jacket sleeves.

10. **In a Pinch**
    "Pinch-an-inch" of extra fabric at each side of the chest, hip, and thigh areas to ensure you select a size that offers a smooth fit with room for natural movement.

Following these tips, you can choose clothes that fit. This is a quick way to enhance your appearance, boost your professional image and bolster self-confidence.

Communicate With a Clear Purpose

When we talk about image, the art of communication is based on keeping your core message intact while presenting it to various audiences. When you communicate effectively, you connect in a relevant way with different groups of people. When you express your image in new ways or to a new audience, it's important to remain committed to your core values. Because communication can happen quickly, it's important to make strategic choices about your communication *style*.

Communication is not only about what you say, it is about what you do. The axiom *"Actions speak louder than words"* says this so well. Your focus is not on creating a disingenuous series of actions or events simply to raise your profile. You want to focus on connecting your values and ideal image qualities with strategic choices to help you position yourself in a clear and relevant way.

Four Powerful Questions You Must Answer

1. Where am I going? KEYWORD: AUTHENTICITY	2. Who am I going to see? KEYWORD: APPROPRIATE
3. How do I want people to experience me? KEYWORD: APPROPRIATE	4. What message will my appearance convey? KEYWORD: ATTRACTIVE

These four inquiries are simple tools for communicating your message from the start of your day. In an *Image Matters* column for the *Indianapolis Business Journal*, I proposed eliminating the term "business casual," which creates confusion, and replacing it with *smart professional*. The four questions provide guidance in considering what you will wear to exude the competency of a professional at work. Although the shift in terminology places the responsibility on you to think through what it means to be a *smart professional* in a particular role, part of this comes from knowing who you are. If you have an aversion to ironing, invest in no-iron shirts and dry clean often. If you can't style your hair fast enough in the morning, consider a new cut. By asking yourself the Four Powerful Questions daily, you provide the valuable inventory necessary to bring your appearance into alignment with that day's goals regardless of the dress code.

Chapter Eight

More Than a Makeover

The thought of a person walking into your closet and telling you what to wear is frightening! With so many shows depicting rapid makeovers full of finger wagging and "fashion don'ts," it's no wonder some people cringe at the idea of talking with an image consultant. What drives the success of ImageCube is my approach to personal development. I know quick fixes can't deliver the quality you deserve.

I use proven tools, including an in-depth personality assessment, and more than an hour of discussion and review to help people like you clarify and define their ultimate message. The result is an alignment between who you are on the inside, and what the world sees on the outside. At ImageCube, I help people create the kind of harmony which makes every interaction with friends, family, and coworkers more authentic.

Real People with Real Results

Few people wake up looking like supermodels. After all, we're only human. While we may not start the day looking our best, most of us want to walk out the door ready to take on the world and share our best image with those we meet throughout the day. Understanding the power of first impressions gives us ample reason to make sure the person we present is exactly who we want people to see.

From Girl-Next-Door to High-Fashion

Working with Sarah M. was fun. Having modeled for several years, she was ready to take her look, and her career, to another level. She wanted to step away from the casual appearance and move toward an edgier, more high-fashion expression. An experienced hairstylist provided a style that was edgy without being severe.

I took into consideration Sarah's personal and professional goals, while determining the best way to frame her heart-shaped face. Once her hair was set, I worked with a makeup artist to highlight her eyes and provide a fresh, youthful look. I was careful to retain the authentic charm which comes naturally to Sarah, while updating her image in an easily maintained way.

Before taking Sarah to a salon, I focused on crafting a visual message that is true to who she is and what she wants. This is why I love what I do at ImageCube – I help people harness the power of their image without losing an ounce of who they are on the inside. Sarah remained approachable and likable, yet now her presentation is better matched to her career. With subtle changes, it may be easier to gain the exposure she desires in her chosen profession.

Style is Personal

Angie is another example of image being about our internal dialogue, not just our external expression:

"I have never been good at putting outfits together and knowing what looks good on me. I don't buy anything because with all the choices, I can't decide, so I get nothing at all. Sola has empowered me to find my own personal style that flatters me yet fits my lifestyle. I have confidence now when dressing and going out."

- Angie L.

The tools I used for Angie are part of a process defined by her needs. I started with the Myers-Briggs Type Indicator (MBTI) to understand her personality. We discovered her definition of "attractive" by reviewing current magazine illustrations. I invited Angie to define the challenges she wanted help addressing as part of a proven process for image management. The results were dramatic for Angie, a caregiver who finally began to find herself.

It's An Honor To Serve You

I love fashion and enjoy seeing colors and textures transform how people see themselves. I've had the honor of guiding client after client in communicating who they are in a calm and confident manner. In the process, they've gained a unique gift: empowerment. Watching how they become more commanding and feel more worthy of the very best is a magical moment. There are many paths to empowerment, from great books to esteemed mentors. The tools I use begin as clothing and become defining elements of vivid personal stories, self-expression and self-care. The gift clients give me is their joy! I know my work is always "more than a makeover."

Personal Reflection Break

With so many factors taking place all at once, it often seems creating a clear and consistent image is a tough challenge. This book is one of your resources. Your next step is to seek the assistance of a certified image consultant and see results in less time than you thought possible.

Thinking of your current image, your Style Code and the information you've gained so far, describe what you would have ImageCube help you do during a one-on-one session.

_____

_____

_____

_____

_____

_____

Understand the ImageCube Difference

The power of image is important, both personally and professionally. Yet, too often it is difficult to find a clear answer about the differences between a personal stylist, personal shopper, and an image consultant. When reinventing, fine-tuning or editing your personal appearance and overall personal style remember one thing I tell my clients:

"Fashion is about what people wear **in general**.
Image is about what you wear **on purpose**."

Here are important questions to ask yourself as you seek professional assistance. All of the answers should be "Yes":

- ✓ Is my consultant certified?
- ✓ Are the processes clear and easy to follow?
- ✓ Does the consultant have relevant experience relating to my goals?
- ✓ Are we working toward a clear vision with a strategic plan for implementation?
- ✓ Are appearance decisions designed to consistently reflect my authentic self?

The following five areas present an easy-to-use filter which protects you from risky fashion advice or quick-fix schemes. Take a moment to invest in yourself. Enjoy the lasting results!

Certification

The leading institution for gaining certification as an image consultant is the Association of Image Consultants International (AICI), which offers three levels of certification. Through clear processes, testing, and in-depth review and analysis, AICI ensures you're in good hands.

Processes

Methods used by consultants vary, but they should provide a clear path for your success. It is the consultant's job to educate, empower, and inspire visible results. Whether the tools are boot camps, training programs, methods such as the **Image³ Style System®**, or one-on-one programs to help you reclaim personal power, be sure your consultant offers solutions with clear objectives and specific steps for success.

Relevance

Selecting a consultant is about professional chemistry and skill. Whether you're reaching for a higher station in a corporation or looking forward to becoming a famous author, the person you work with should bring knowledge and experience to the table. ImageCube is well suited to aid professionals in transition to or from corporate careers. Personally, I have more than a decade of high-level corporate experience paired with a background in sociology and travels in more than 20 countries. I combine my knowledge with cultural and social awareness gained through national and international travel, and my desire to empower professionals to harness their influence.

Vision

An effective consultant helps you identify, define, and act to find your ideal self. Vision-based service focuses on expressing who you are, not who you "should be" according to others' definitions. By helping you define your personal vision, it becomes much easier to find and utilize lines, shapes, colors, patterns, and textures – as elements of clothing design – to bring the package to life. So rather than trying on 300 garments, you might consider 60, but they all clearly support the message of your "look" as it relates to your vision.

In the words of ImageCube clients, the difference sounds like this:

- *"I've never thought this much about the message I'm sending through my choices in clothing."*

- *"Flipping through a magazine has never been the same. I feel so much more empowered."*

- *"I let the message I must communicate dictate what I wear during the week. My weekends are for play and I want to communicate a more relaxed and casual message."*

- *"I didn't know there was so much to learn about fashion. This will make a huge difference with how I shop going forward."*

When the vision is clear and a talented consultant delivers a job well done, you gain tools to use time and again. You are empowered through image awareness.

Consistent

Although trends come and go, the core components of your authentic self are reliable over time. Consistent results are based on making choices reflecting who you are. Forget all the "reality shows" depicting people throwing out all their clothes during a wardrobe makeover. Your personal style comes more naturally when it is a consistent reflection of who you are even when you change jobs, cities, or weekend hobbies. Eventually, you are known for "your look" and you'll know it all started with the right certified image consultant.

Create Your Plan

Your goal is to set a date for your own image renewal. There's no need to ask where your inspiration will come from or how you'll figure it all out because with ImageCube you have a partner who is by your side the entire time. I've created a solution to make shopping, planning, and updating your wardrobe as easy as powering your smart phone – literally. My ongoing mission is to provide solutions to empower and strengthen you with tools built specifically *for* you.

What made an impact on you as you read this book? Those points are your first set of tools as you refine your image. By writing it down, you do more than observe the information, you become an owner of it and you help ImageCube do more than offer solutions. You make the solutions real and personally meaningful. Let's make a lasting impact with a personal recap, based on what you captured in this book.

What ideas did you underline in RED to implement in the next 7 to 14 days?

_____

_____

_____

_____

_____
_____
_____
_____
_____
_____
_____

What ideas did you underline in BLUE to implement in the next 1 to 3 months?

_____
_____
_____
_____
_____
_____
_____
_____

How many magazine illustrations have you saved which you believe capture your best image?

_____
_____
_____
_____
_____

Your Next Step

The amount of trust given to ImageCube to help you navigate new and sudden changes is immense. When I finally step into your closet, I'm by your side, not pointing my finger or furrowing my brow. For every garment we touch there's a story. There is a reason why, at one time, a certain color, texture or style spoke to you in a meaningful way. As much as people might think it's about throwing out the old and bringing in the new, it's really about helping you reconnect with your true self.

If *you're* ready to look and feel great in all aspects of your life, connect with ImageCube today. There is no reason to leave passion for later. This is your life and it's time to live it more fully! ImageCube doesn't just help you find clothes, trends or new styles, it helps you rediscover yourself and finally express your truly authentic, appropriate, and attractive self. Visit ImageCube's website or pick up the phone for your complimentary 15-minute consultation to determine exactly how ImageCube can empower you.

Sola Adelowo
Clarity. Confidence. Growth.

www.imagecubellc.com
Call now: 317.529.0946

Be Confident & Style Savvy Bootcamp

Would you like your appearance to effectively work *for* you? Do you feel like you're stuck in a style rut? Are you ready to find <u>lasting solutions</u> to improve your image?

Join us at **Be Confident and Style Savvy Bootcamp** with **Sola Adelowo** and get what you've been looking for! Experience how the Image^3 Style System will help you redefine your style vocabulary and raise your fashion confidence, for good!

During the Bootcamp, you will:

- Define your Style Code and better communicate who you are in pursuit of your goals.
- Design a look that's comfortable, confident and appropriate and that also retains your personal flair.
- Assess your basic wardrobe pieces to better suit your goals or fit your lifestyle.
- Create a plan to find the key elements you still need to complete your wardrobe.
- Create systems to look your best for any occasion with ease and consistency.

What you get when you join this amazing bootcamp:

- Small group size of just 8 people ensures a personal focus and direct communication.
- Nine hours of Training, Education, and Personal Insight over three days.
- Custom Personality Type Assessment (MBTI).
- The opportunity to meet like-minded people and define your personal brand and style.
- Living a life that is more *you* by learning how to make a great impression look effortless every time.

Visit www.ImageCubeLLC.com to sign-up for our next bootcamp program. Contact sola@imagecubellc.com to request a bootcamp program for your organization or workplace.

Praise for Sola & the Image Style System®

"I learned so much about myself and how to make a style statement for many different occasions with Sola's expert consulting. Sola helped shift my paradigm regarding fashion and I feel I have so many more options to work with in my wardrobe now and in the future. It was a great investment I made in myself!"

- Liz Snyder, Vice President Human Resources,
Damar Services, Inc.

"I found Sola to be many things. Inspirational, thought provoking, informative are some of the words that come to mind. I really never thought of dress the way you presented it. I enjoyed your presentation style as well. I could clearly see your successful business background. That was unexpected but really helpful to the way you presented ideas. I guess I'm now a raving fan!"

- David Phoebus, Indianapolis Chapter Chairman,
Financial Executives Networking Group

"I love fashion but hate shopping which means I rarely go to stores to try stuff on, and I usually shop over the internet. Sometimes I am influenced by a trend that doesn't fit my style, age or body type, but I'll try to wear it anyway. Usually, I wear it once and I'm done. Sola helped me understand why I like what I like by going through my closet and looking at the pieces I wear often and comparing them to those that may be stylish, but I just don't wear. The process was invaluable. Now I know what to look for and why!"

- Katherine C. Nagler, Director of Development,
The Health Foundation of Greater Indianapolis

"The Be Confident & Style Savvy Bootcamp was a major breakthrough for me. Sola was so knowledgeable and helpful in guiding me through the personal image discovery process. I would highly recommend the bootcamp to everyone. It's a great program for anyone who wants to live a more fulfilling, productive, and happier life."

- Karyn Oyler, Human Resource Professional

"Through working with Sola, I was able to understand my personal style and define a process for appearing stylish yet appropriate. I feel more confident identifying clothes that show my personality and support the image I want to present to the world."
- Julie M. Carmichael, System Vice-Presdent & Chief Strategy Officer,
St. Vincent Health

"The Be Confident & Style Savvy Bootcamp helped me to think about how my audience, what I want to convey, my role, and my personality -- ALL play a part in deciding what to wear."
- Stacy Fletcher, Independent Advocare Consultant

"In the bootcamp, it was just as helpful to evaluate my outfit and what my clothes were communicating as it was to evaluate the other guests' outfits. Learning from different guests' perspectives and experiences was eye opening. Plus, Sola's process to determine my target audience and what my clothes need to communicate clarified for me how I need to show-up."
- Diana Maxam, ProMed Medical Management

References

Arnell, Peter, Steve Kettmann, and Martha Stewart E. *Shift: How to Reinvent Your Business, Your Career, and Your Personal Brand.* New York: Broadway, 2010. Print.

Adelowo, Sola. "Image Matters: Biggest Business Casual Problem Is Its Tricky Definition" *Indianapolis Business Journal.* January 19, 2013: pg. 30.

Beals, Jeff. *Self Marketing Power: Branding Yourself as a Business of One.* Omaha, NE: Keynote Pub., 2008. Print.

Bixler, Susan, and Nancy Nix-Rice. *The New Professional Image.* Avon, MA: Adams Media, 2005. Print.

Buckingham, Marcus, and Donald Clifton O. *Now, Discover Your Strengths.* New York: Free, 2001. Print.

Cahill, Jonathan. *Igniting the Brand: Strategies That Have Shot Brands to Success.* London, U.K.: Marshall Cavendish, 2008. Print.

Calasibetta, Charlotte Mankey., and Phyllis Tortora G. *The Fairchild Dictionary of Fashion.* New York: Fairchild Publications, 2003. Print.

Charlton, Fascitelli Melanie., and Kevin Clark. *Shop Your Closet: The Ultimate Guide to Organizing Your Closet with Style.* New York: Collins, 2008. Print.

Davis, Marian L. *Visual Design in Dress.* 3rd ed. Upper Saddle River, NJ: Prentice Hall, 1996. Print.

Farr, Kendall. *Style Evolution: How to Create Ageless Personal Style in Your 40s and beyond.* New York: Gotham, 2009. Print.

Farr, Kendall. *The Pocket Stylist: Behind-the-scenes Expertise from a Fashion Pro on Creating Your Own Unique Look*. New York, NY: Gotham, 2004. Print.

Gross, Kim Johnson., Jeff Stone, and Kristina Zimbalist. *Dress Smart--women: Wardrobes That Win in the New Workplace*. New York: Warner, 2002. Print.

Hodgkinson, Susan. *The Leader's Edge: Using Personal Branding to Drive Performance and Profit*. New York: IUniverse, 2005. Print.

Huszczo, Gregory E. *Making a Difference by Being Yourself: Using Your Personality Type at Work and in Relationships*. Mountain View, CA: Davies-Black Pub., 2009. Print.

Johnson, Kim K. P., and Sharron Lennon J. *Appearance and Power*. Oxford: Berg, 1999. Print.

Kaiser, Susan B. *The Social Psychology of Clothing: Symbolic Appearances in Context*. New York: Fairchild Publications, 1997. Print.

Kinsel, Brenda. *Dowdy to Diva: Brenda Kinsel's 30-day Makeover*. San Francisco: Chronicle, 2007. Print.

Maxwell, John C. *Talent Is Never Enough: Discover the Choices That Will Take You beyond Your Talent*. Nashville, TN: Thomas Nelson, 2007. Print.

McCarthy, Carrie, Danielle LaPorte, and Gregory Crow. *Style Statement: Live by Your Own Design*. New York: Little, Brown and, 2008. Print.

McNally, David, and Karl Speak D. *Be Your Own Brand: A Breakthrough Formula for Standing out from the Crowd*. San Francisco, CA: Berrett-Koehler, 2003. Print.

Mizrahi, Isaac. *How to Have Style*. New York: Penguin Group, 2008. Print.

Neumeier, Marty. *The Designful Company: How to Build a Culture of Nonstop Innovation : A Whiteboard Overview*. Berkeley, CA: New Riders, 2009. Print.

Peters, Thomas J. *Reinventing Work: The Brand You 50, Or, Fifty Ways to Transform Yourself from an Employee into a Brand That Shouts Distinction, Commitment, and Passion!* New York: Knopf, 1999. Print.

Rasband, Judith. *Fabulous Fit*. New York: Fairchild, 2005. Print.

Rasband, Judith. *Wardrobe Strategies for Women*. New York: Fairchild Publications, 2002. Print.

Spillane, Mary, and Christine Sherlock. *Color Me Beautiful's Looking Your Best: Color, Makeup, and Style*. Lanham: Madison, 1995. Print.

Volin, Kathryn J. *Buff and Polish: A Practical Guide to Enhance Your Professional Image and Communication Style*. Minneapolis, MN: Pentagon Pub., 1999. Print.

Yanez, Shirley. "Fashionista versus Stylista" *More Magazine*. June 2010. Web. 25 April 2013.

www.keirsey.com/sorter/register.aspx (last visited April 1, 2013)

About the Author

Sola Adelowo, Founder of ImageCube
& Public Speaker

When you consider the power of
presentation you know there's more to
getting dressed than simply putting on
clothes.

Sola's instinctive awareness, combined
with her unique life experiences led her
to launch ImageCube to help people
harness the power of image. Born in
Dallas, Texas, to Nigerian parents, Sola was raised for much of her
childhood in Nigeria while her parents received their undergraduate and
graduate degrees in the U.S. Her cultural experiences included clothing that
was most often handmade by a tailor. Through family connections such as
her maternal grandmother, a fabric merchant, and paternal grandparents
who were active in the community, Sola gained knowledge of how
powerful image can be at an early age. Fine fabrics, talented tailors, and
colorful, well-tailored clothing helped to shape her interest in the power of
beautiful, purposeful, and personalized clothing.

With a BA in Sociology from Wellesley College, MBA coursework from
Post University, and more than a decade in the corporate world from
Boston, Chicago and Indianapolis, Sola brings intuitive knowledge, a
practical awareness of corporate culture, and proven research and theory to
her ImageCube clients.

She is a certified image consultant of the Association of Image Consultants
International (AICI), a certified Myers-Brigg Personality Type Practitioner,
the fashion-and-image contributor for *Indy Style* on Indianapolis-area CBS-
affiliate WISH TV-8, and contributed as the *Image Matters* columnist for the

Indianapolis Business Journal. She also has been a featured fashion expert on the *Fox 59 Morning News Show* and *The Indianapolis Recorder's Recorder-On-Air-Report.* Through a series of promotions at Chubb Specialty Insurance Company, Sola came to Indianapolis as an Underwriting Manager who was charged with developing staff and leading a multi-million- dollar operation that specialized in employment and directors liability insurance. Sola's venture into the fashion industry has included being the executive director and co-producer of Midwest Fashion Week where she was instrumental in expanding the fashion week's breadth of programming and brand visibility. Sola lives her vision every day by serving as Personal Development Chairperson for Junior League of Indianapolis.